INTRODUCTION T

MATHS

Nigel Langdon and Janet Cook

Designed by Kim Blundell and Sue Mims

**Illustrated by Jane Andrews, Jeremy Banks, Martin Newton
Simon Roulstone, Chris Lyon, Iain Ashman
and Naomi Reed**

Computer programs by Chris Oxlade

Edited by Lisa Watts

WITH COMPUTER PROGRAM LISTINGS

Contents

First published in 1984 by Usborne Publishing Ltd, 83-85 Saffron Hill, London EC1 8RT, England.

Printed in Belgium

What is maths?

The word mathematics comes from the Greek word *manthanein* meaning to learn. This is a clue to what maths is all about. For more than 4000 years, from the building of the pyramids to the designing of a modern motorway intersection, people have been studying the relationships between shapes and numbers to help them to learn about and organize the world we live in.

Orbiting satellites in space, repeating patterns in the design of wallpaper, driving a car – all depend upon the mathematics of shape, number and precision. What connects these different features is logic, and studying maths can help you to think more clearly and logically.

The best way to understand maths is to take a pencil and paper (or a calculator) and try things out for yourself. There are a number of puzzles scattered throughout this book which you can do to test yourself. The answers are on pages 46-47.

If you are not familiar with them, mathematical symbols may look a bit frightening. In fact, they are just a shorthand way of writing simple statements. Once you have learned the basics, you will find it easier to understand the more complicated ideas. So don't expect to understand everything at once; tackle small sections at a time.

Some of the puzzles in the book have red stars showing the number of points you can award yourself if you get the answer right. Keep a record of your score. Then, when you have done all the puzzles, look at the score chart at the back of the book to see how well you did. If you get top marks, you're a super mathematician!

On page 45, there are some simple computer programs to test mathematical theories such as probability. The programs will work on most types of home computer. If you have, or can borrow, a computer, try them out – they are very short and take only a few minutes to type in.

The world of numbers

Can you imagine a world without numbers? Numbers are such an important part of everyday conversation that it would be extremely difficult to go shopping or tell the time without using them. Think of any recent developments in modern technology, for example satellites, lasers or cable television; they would have been impossible without the science of numbers.

How many?

The answer to the question "How many?" is always a number. Yet numbers on their own can be very misleading.

How far is Austria from France?

5

1

200

125

The answers are all correct. Can you think of words which could accompany each of these numbers?*

Which one?

Numbers are also used for labelling and identification. Buses are labelled so that all those on the same route have the same number. But each vehicle has a different registration number so that it can be identified.

367

Counting in tens . . .

There have been numerous ways of counting in the past, yet almost all of them are based upon counting in tens. This is possibly because most people count on their fingers at some time.

Aborigines of South Australia use a word for 10 which also means "two hands".

. . . and hundreds and thousands

Most of the ancient number systems had different symbols for units, tens, hundreds and thousands. Can you translate this Egyptian number?

1

The order is not important, neither is the position of the symbols on the page.

I = 1
∩ = 10
ℓ = 100
𝄐 = 1000

Egyptian number

3

C and M are the first letters of *centum* and *mille*, the Latin words for hundred and thousand.

ROMA
MCXX

Later, Romans used V for 5 and L for 50.

MCM CXXX IV

It was not until the Middle Ages that Latin scholars used IV to mean 4 (one less than 5). How would you translate CM?

4

In Northern Japan, the ancient Ainu language uses *wan* (meaning "two-sided") for 10.

The symbols we use to write numbers are called digits, coming from the Latin for finger.

2 The Romans used I, X, C and M. The symbols I and X (1 and 10) probably came from a much earlier method of writing numbers when cuts were made on a wooden stick.

What is the value of this number?

4

One of the 2s on this sign means 2000 and the other is only 2. Which is which?

India 2192

Our modern decimal system, developed in India by AD 570, is the most sophisticated of all. It is possible to write any number using only ten digits. This is because of the importance given to the order of writing the digits; for example 27 is a different number from 72.*

Pictures by numbers

Just as a colouring book can tell you which colours to use, the pictures sent back to Earth by space ships and satellites are transmitted by numbers.

A Mariner spacecraft which is photographing a planet takes television pictures. Each tiny square of the picture is examined by an on-board computer and given a number between 0 and 63 to indicate its brightness. These numbers are signalled back to Earth and another computer then uses them to reconstruct the picture.

Digital noughts and crosses

A good variation on the game noughts and crosses is to use the digits 1 to 9.

Each digit may be used only once in a game. The winner is the first person to make a line of three numbers which total 10.

3 1
2
7

Is there a biggest number?

Imagine a very, very large number – the largest you can think of. Can you add 1 to it?

Mathematicians use the symbol ∞ (infinity) to represent quantities which could never be counted, even if you counted for ever.

A dead 8!

5

*Go to pages 6-7 for more about the decimal system.

Decimals

The decimal system allows us to write any whole number using a combination of up to ten different symbols: 0,1,2,3,4,5,6,7,8 and 9. The value of each symbol changes according to its position in the number.

This seven means seven hundreds.

This seven means seven tens.

1000s	100s	10s	1s
	9	9	9
			1 +
1	0	0	0

Reading from the right, the first digit shows the number of 1s, the second digit the number of 10s and so on. You can count up to 9 before moving to the next position.

Decimal fractions

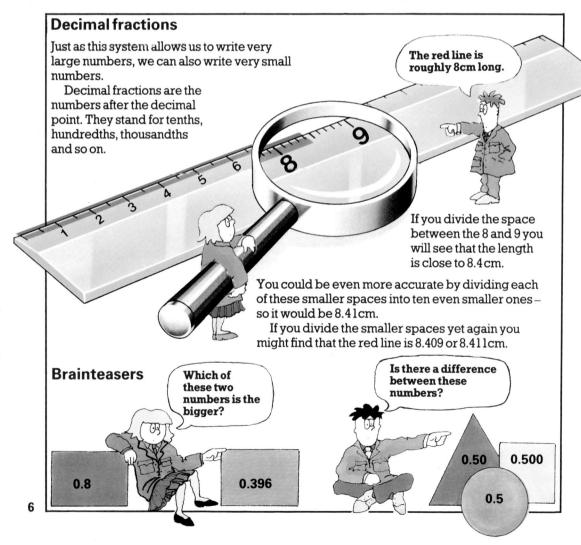

Just as this system allows us to write very large numbers, we can also write very small numbers.

Decimal fractions are the numbers after the decimal point. They stand for tenths, hundredths, thousandths and so on.

The red line is roughly 8cm long.

If you divide the space between the 8 and 9 you will see that the length is close to 8.4cm.

You could be even more accurate by dividing each of these smaller spaces into ten even smaller ones – so it would be 8.41cm.

If you divide the smaller spaces yet again you might find that the red line is 8.409 or 8.411cm.

Brainteasers

Which of these two numbers is the bigger?

0.8

0.396

Is there a difference between these numbers?

0.50   0.500

0.5

6

Rounding off

Although decimal fractions make it possible to count to the minutest detail, for most purposes working with three significant figures is accurate enough.

At a marathon race where the crowd totalled 156 432, a reporter might write that there were 156 000 spectators.

2 398   7.2153

Can you round off these numbers?

Rules for rounding off

To round off a number to three significant figures, first check the fourth figure.

a) If it is below 5, use the first 3 figures and replace the rest with 0s.

b) If it is 5 or above, increase the figure on its left by 1 before replacing the rest with 0s.

Moving the decimal point

The two numbers below are roughly 300 and 3, so the first number is 100 times larger than the second.

$$297.4 \overset{\times\,100}{\underset{\div\,100}{\rightleftarrows}} 2.974$$

When you multiply 2.974 by 100 it looks as though the decimal point jumps two places to the right.

Dividing by decimals

When dividing by decimals without a calculator it is easier to move the decimal points so that both the numbers you are working with are whole numbers.

$35 \div 0.7$ is the same as $350 \div 7$.

In fact, is it the decimal point or the number which moves?

DECIMAL POINT MOVES:

÷ 10	1 place left
÷ 100	2 places left
÷ 1000	3 places left
X 10	1 place right
X 100	2 places right
X 1000	3 places right

When you are multiplying and dividing on a calculator it is easy to press a wrong key. Use this guide to check that your answer is roughly what you expected.

Dice game

This is a game for two players who take it in turns to throw a dice.

The first player to cover three numbers in a line is the winner.

Multiply any number from this table by your dice score.

See if there is a number which matches your answer on the board on the right and cover it.

2·5	3	0·05
1·5	2	0·75
0·5	1	0·25

		3	15	12	3
0·25	2·5	3	0·75	1·5	5
6	2	2·5	1	6	0·05
1·5	0·5	1·25	1	2	0·75
1	3	0·25	0·5	1	
0·2	1·5	6	4·5	3	1
1·5	12	2	7·5	1·5	4

Zero and negatives

What is zero? Is it nothing or is it something? Can you have less than zero? The answers may seem obvious to us now, but they puzzled early mathematicians. Because of this, the use of a zero symbol originated quite late in mathematics and it was not until the Middle Ages that it was introduced into Europe from India.

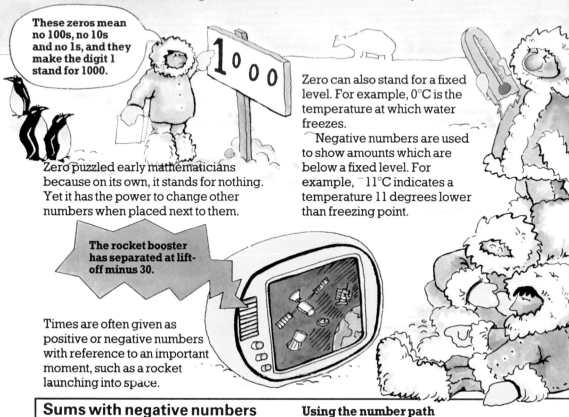

These zeros mean no 100s, no 10s and no 1s, and they make the digit 1 stand for 1000.

Zero puzzled early mathematicians because on its own, it stands for nothing. Yet it has the power to change other numbers when placed next to them.

Zero can also stand for a fixed level. For example, 0°C is the temperature at which water freezes.

Negative numbers are used to show amounts which are below a fixed level. For example, ⁻11°C indicates a temperature 11 degrees lower than freezing point.

The rocket booster has separated at lift-off minus 30.

Times are often given as positive or negative numbers with reference to an important moment, such as a rocket launching into space.

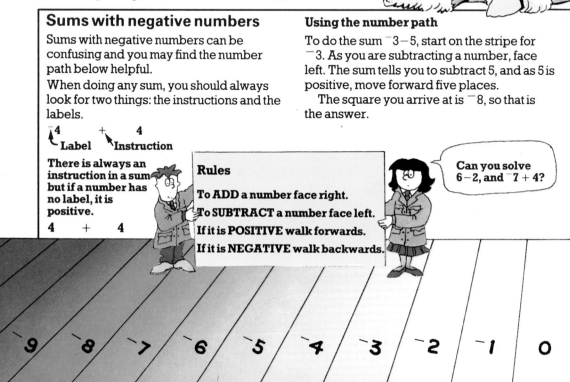

Sums with negative numbers

Sums with negative numbers can be confusing and you may find the number path below helpful.

When doing any sum, you should always look for two things: the instructions and the labels.

⁻4   +   4
Label   Instruction

There is always an instruction in a sum but if a number has no label, it is positive.

4   +   4

Using the number path

To do the sum ⁻3−5, start on the stripe for ⁻3. As you are subtracting a number, face left. The sum tells you to subtract 5, and as 5 is positive, move forward five places.

The square you arrive at is ⁻8, so that is the answer.

Rules

To **ADD** a number face right.

To **SUBTRACT** a number face left.

If it is **POSITIVE** walk forwards.

If it is **NEGATIVE** walk backwards.

Can you solve 6−2, and ⁻7 + 4?

⁻9 ⁻8 ⁻7 ⁻6 ⁻5 ⁻4 ⁻3 ⁻2 ⁻1 0

Vectors

One of the important uses of negative numbers is in work with vectors. Vectors are quantities which are represented by arrows to show their direction and size.

A rocket which is travelling at 80km per second towards the west could be represented like this. The length of the arrow shows the size of velocity (speed).

Another rocket, travelling at 60km per second due east would be shown like this. The negative symbol means it is travelling in the opposite direction to the first rocket.

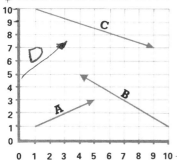

On a grid system like this, vectors are referred to by two numbers. Vector A is $\binom{4}{2}$ because it goes 4 squares right and 2 squares up. What are vectors B and C?

Vector puzzle

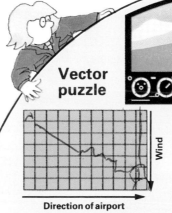

Direction of airport

A pilot needs to fly due east for an hour to reach the next airport, but there is a strong wind of 100km per hour blowing from the north.

If he steers towards the airport, the wind will blow him too far south. Can you use this vector diagram to find out the direction in which the pilot should steer?

Multiplication

You can also use the path to do multiplication because when you multiply you are in fact adding up (or if the first number is negative, subtracting) several times. The only difference is that you should start on 0.

$$3 \times 5 = (0) + 5 + 5 + 5 = 15$$
$$3 \times {}^-5 = (0) + {}^-5 + {}^-5 + {}^-5 = {}^-15$$
$${}^-3 \times {}^-5 = (0) - {}^-5 - {}^-5 - {}^-5 = 15$$

Try these sums on the path:
$2 \times {}^-3$, ${}^-4 \times {}^-2$, and 1×3.

Quick tips

If you check your answers, you will find that the following rules always apply:

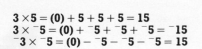

2   3   4   5   6   7   8   9

Use your head

You don't need to be a genius to be good at mathematics. What you do need is a familiarity with numbers and shapes. This helps you to recognize patterns amongst them and is much better than trying to remember lots of rules by heart. On these two pages there are tips to help you multiply and divide.

There is no set way to calculate with numbers; you should decide for yourself which method allows you to find the correct answer most easily. Can you think of more short cuts yourself?

2, 4 and 8

To multiply by 4, just double the number and double the answer.
Example: 21×4

$$21 \times 2 = 42$$
$$42 \times 2 = 84$$

so 21×4 must be 84.

To multiply by 8, double the number three times.
Example: 12×8

$$12 \times 2 = 24$$
$$24 \times 2 = 48$$
$$48 \times 2 = 96$$

so $12 \times 8 = 96$

Dividing is the opposite of multiplying, so to divide by 4, halve the number and halve again. What is $128 \div 8$?

Fairground number cruncher

Someone who was very clever at working out simple methods to solve complicated problems was George Bidder, who became a famous fairground entertainer. In 1815, at the age of nine, he took less than a minute to answer this question:

The moon is 123 256 miles from Earth and sound travels at the speed of 4 miles a minute. How long would it be before someone on the moon could hear an explosion on Earth?

21 days
9 hours
and 34 minutes

Multiply by 9

Look at the nine times table:

$$1 \times 9 = 9$$
$$2 \times 9 = 18$$
$$3 \times 9 = 27$$
$$4 \times 9 = 36$$
$$5 \times 9 = 45$$
$$6 \times 9 = 54$$
$$7 \times 9 = 63$$
$$8 \times 9 = 72$$
$$9 \times 9 = 81$$
$$10 \times 9 = 90$$

$1 + 8 = 9$

$2 + 7 = 9$

The two digits in the answers always add up to 9. Does this happen when you multiply large numbers by 9?

$$53 \times 9 = 477$$

$$4 + 7 + 7 = 18$$
$$\text{and } 1 + 8 = 9$$

It takes two stages but the digits still add up to 9. This is a useful check and is also helpful if you want to divide by 9. Is 684 divisible by 9?

Multiply by 11

The 11 times table is probably the easiest to recognize:

$$22, 33, 44, 55, 66, 77, 88, 99 \ldots$$

Here is a quick way to multiply 11 by a two figure number whose digits add up to less than 10.

$$27 \times 11 = 297$$

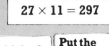

Add the 2 and the 7.

Put the answer in between.

Try it with some other numbers.

Computer brain

546372891

In today's world of calculators and computers the human brain can still work amazingly quickly. Shakuntala Devi's is probably the fastest in the world. She lives in Bangalore in India, but spends much of her time travelling around the world giving demonstrations of her ability.

In one famous lecture in Texas, she was asked to find the number which, when multiplied by itself 23 times, gave this answer:

9167486769200391580986609275853801624831066801443086
2240712651642793465704086709659327920576748080679002
2783016354924852380335745316935111903596577547340075
6816883056208210161291328455468057801588806771

Shakuntala worked it out in fifty seconds. In order to check her answer, students used a Univac 1108 computer. It took the computer one full minute to confirm she was right – but it had to be given more than 13 000 instructions first.

Multiply by 10

To multiply by 10, just add a nought to change the position of the digits.

Example: 25×10

$$25 \times 10$$
$$250$$

To multiply any number by 100, just add two noughts . . .

$$32 \times 100$$
$$3200$$

. . .because multiplying by 100 is the same as multiplying by 10 twice. How would you multiply by 1000?

Multiply by 15

To multiply by 15, you need to recognize that 15 is 10 + half of 10.

Example: 32×15

32×10	=	320
32×5	=	160

Add the two answers: 480

So 32×15 must equal 480.

Try working out these sums:

a) 8×15
b) 36×15
c) 92×15

Beat the teacher

When the teacher of Karl Gauss wanted to keep his class quiet for an hour, he set them questions like the one opposite.

Most of Karl's classmates worked them out slowly on their slates, but Karl, who was only nine, came up with the answers in seconds.

Karl, born in 1777, was to become one of the greatest mathematicians ever. He used a neat trick to solve this sum. Can you see what it was? And find the answer?

Work out the sum of $1 + 2 + 3$ . . . up to 1000.

Psst: $1 + 1000$, $2 + 999$, $3 + 998$, etc. all equal 1001.

Shapes everywhere

Mathematics is often called the science of numbers, but that is less than half of it. It is just as much to do with studying shapes and classifying them into particular groups. Once you have done this you can find rules which will apply to solving problems for any shape in the group.

Everything in the world has a shape, from the most intricate snowflake to a skyscraper. The easiest shapes to classify have straight lines, and you can find out about them on these two pages.

How tall?
How many leaves?
Leaf shape?

The organization of things into groups is important in many other subjects, for example in the identification of a tree species.

Classifying shapes

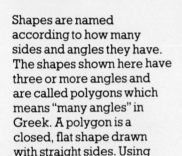

Shapes are named according to how many sides and angles they have. The shapes shown here have three or more angles and are called polygons which means "many angles" in Greek. A polygon is a closed, flat shape drawn with straight sides. Using the list below, can you name these polygons?

Triangle means three-angled (Latin)
Quadrilateral means four-sided (Latin)
Pentagon means five-angled (Greek)
Hexagon means six-angled (Greek)

Go to pages 18-19 for a study of three-dimensional objects and more complicated shapes.

Regular polygons

This is the headquarters of the American defence forces.

A regular polygon is one in which all the angles and sides are the same.

How many sides would a polygon need before it became a circle?

Do you know what it is called?

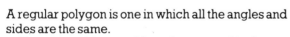

pentagon

The family of triangles

Triangles can be grouped according to their sides.

A scalene triangle has all sides different in length.

An isosceles triangle has two sides the same in length.

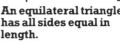

Can you draw a triangle whose sides are 5cm, 3cm and 9cm?

An equilateral triangle has all sides equal in length.

Squares and rectangles

It is not so easy to organize four-sided polygons into groups.

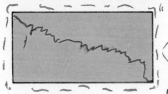

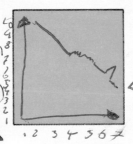

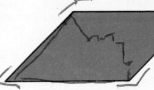

A rectangle is a quadrilateral which has square corners and whose opposite sides are parallel . . .

. . . but that makes a square a rectangle too.

A parallelogram has opposite sides parallel as well, so that makes a square a parallelogram too.

The same shape

◀ Are these two shapes the same? If you picked up the one on the right, turned it over and placed it on top of the shape on the left, you would find that they fitted together exactly. This means that they are congruent because they have identical sides and angles.

This shape is not congruent to those on the left but its shape is the same. It is an enlargement of the shape and so, mathematically speaking, it is similar.

Fitting shapes

You can make very attractive patterns (called tessellations) by placing different shapes side by side. The Romans used to decorate their walls and floors with "tessellae", which were tiny pieces of mosaic.

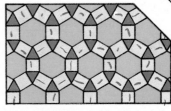

Which three regular polygons were used to create the tessellation above?

13

Measuring surfaces

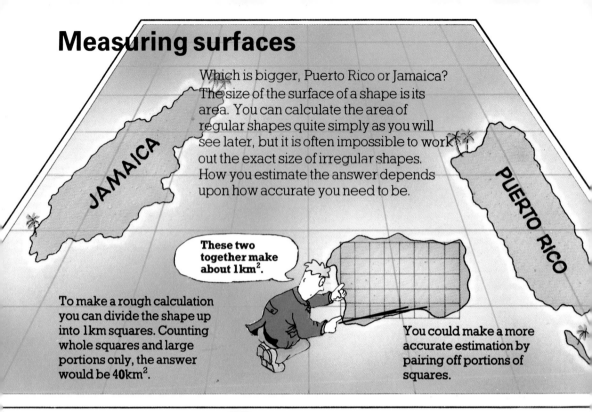

Which is bigger, Puerto Rico or Jamaica? The size of the surface of a shape is its area. You can calculate the area of regular shapes quite simply as you will see later, but it is often impossible to work out the exact size of irregular shapes. How you estimate the answer depends upon how accurate you need to be.

These two together make about 1km².

To make a rough calculation you can divide the shape up into 1km squares. Counting whole squares and large portions only, the answer would be 40km².

You could make a more accurate estimation by pairing off portions of squares.

Rectangular areas

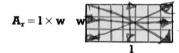

$A_r = l \times w$

If the shape is a rectangle you can count up the squares more quickly by multiplying the length by the width. The area of this rectangle is $7 \times 3 = 21$ squares.

So the formula to calculate the area of a rectangle is $A_r = l \times w$. What do the letters represent?

Rearranging crosses

It is often easier to find the area of a complicated shape by cutting it up and rearranging it to form a more regular outline. The shape still has the same area, as it has just been put together in a different way.

▶If you cut this cross along the red lines you can rearrange it to form the square on the right. You can then use the rectangle formula to find its area.

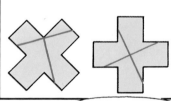

◀Trace these two crosses and cut around the outlines and along the red lines. Now fit the pieces together. You will find that they also form squares.

Units of measurement

Centimetre squares (cm²) or square inches are used to measure the area of small items like floor tiles.

Square metres (m²) or square yards are the best size for measuring pieces of material.

Area formulae

Because rearranging a shape does not change its area, you can use the rectangle formula when calculating the areas of other shapes.

1. Parallelograms

If you cut off one end of a parallelogram on a line at right angles to its sides and stick this at the other end, you will make a rectangle.

> This line is perpendicular to the base because it is at right angles to it.

$$A_p = l \times b$$

> The p in the formula stands for parallelogram.

The area of a parallelogram is the same as the area of a rectangle which has the same side length (l) and the same perpendicular width (b).

2. Triangles

You can draw a rectangle around any triangle using one of the sides as the base of the rectangle.

The base is called b. The height of the rectangle is the same as the height of the triangle from that base.

$$A_t = \tfrac{1}{2}(b \times h)$$

> Trace the shapes and cut them out to check that they make two equal triangles.

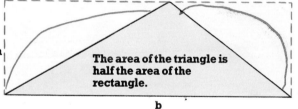

The area of the triangle is half the area of the rectangle.

3. Quadrilaterals

Any quadrilateral can be cut into two triangles, so you can calculate its area in two parts.

$$A_q = \text{Area of triangle A}$$
$$\text{plus}$$
$$\text{Area of triangle B}$$

Puzzle ③

> How would you find the area of this plan of a sports centre?

> Kilometre squares (km^2) or square miles would be used by a geographer measuring the area of an island.

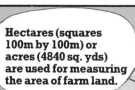

> Hectares (squares 100m by 100m) or acres (4840 sq. yds) are used for measuring the area of farm land.

Circles

Ever tried drinking out of a square mug . . .

. . . or cycling on hexagonal wheels . . .

. . . or using a telephone with a triangular dial?

A circle is a very special shape; it has no corners and any point on its outline (called its circumference) is always the same distance from its central point. This is of great practical use as you can see. It also makes it possible to find a formula to calculate a circle's circumference and area.

Measuring the circle

People have known for centuries that when a wheel turned a complete circle, it always moved forward just over three times its diameter.

$C = \pi d \text{ or } 2\pi r$

In fact, it is about 3.14 times. The number cannot be written exactly, but because of its importance it has been given a name of its own: the Greek letter π (pronounced pie). So to find a circle's circumference, multiply its diameter (or twice the radius) by 3.14.

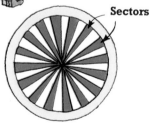

Sectors

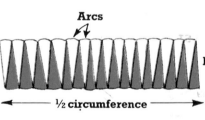

Arcs

Radius

½ circumference

$A = \pi r^2$

If you slice a circle into small sectors you can rearrange the circle approximately as a rectangle. Half the arcs are at the top and half are at the bottom.

The width of the rectangle is approximately the radius of the circle, and the length of the rectangle is almost half the circumference. So the area of the circle is $\pi r \times r$ or πr^2.

Circumference

Arc

Radius

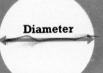

Diameter

Circular shapes

The cone, cylinder and sphere all have curved surfaces. If you cut straight across any one of them on a line parallel to its base, you would find a circle.

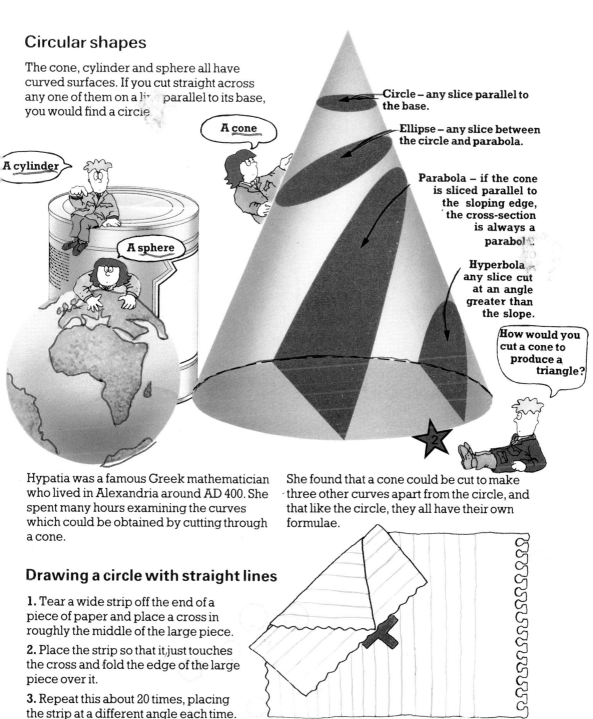

A cone

A cylinder

A sphere

Circle – any slice parallel to the base.

Ellipse – any slice between the circle and parabola.

Parabola – if the cone is sliced parallel to the sloping edge, the cross-section is always a parabola.

Hyperbola – any slice cut at an angle greater than the slope.

How would you cut a cone to produce a triangle?

Hypatia was a famous Greek mathematician who lived in Alexandria around AD 400. She spent many hours examining the curves which could be obtained by cutting through a cone.

She found that a cone could be cut to make three other curves apart from the circle, and that like the circle, they all have their own formulae.

Drawing a circle with straight lines

1. Tear a wide strip off the end of a piece of paper and place a cross in roughly the middle of the large piece.

2. Place the strip so that it just touches the cross and fold the edge of the large piece over it.

3. Repeat this about 20 times, placing the strip at a different angle each time.

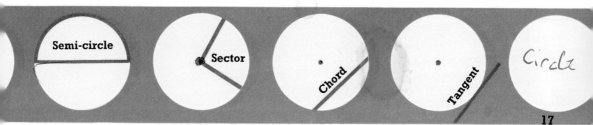

Semi-circle

Sector

Chord

Tangent

Circle

17

3-D

Because we live in a three-dimensional world we are dealing with solid shapes a great deal of the time. However, most people still find it difficult to handle these shapes in their heads as it is easy for the brain to be deceived.

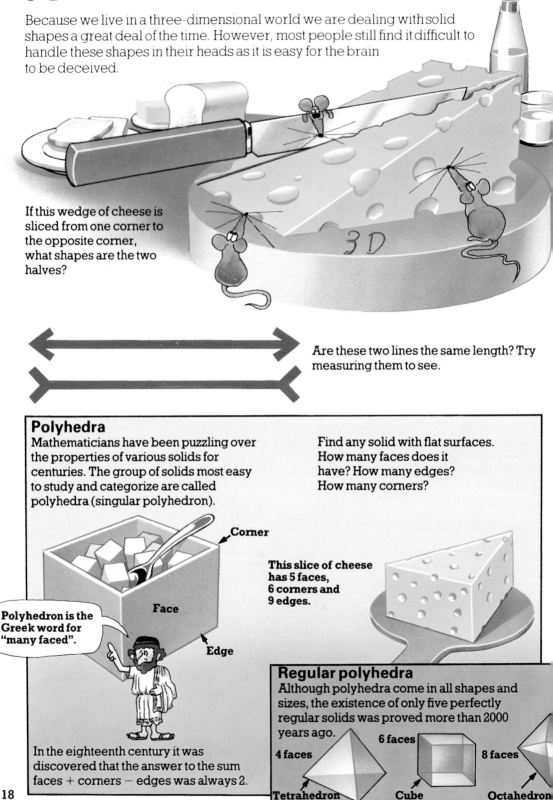

If this wedge of cheese is sliced from one corner to the opposite corner, what shapes are the two halves?

Are these two lines the same length? Try measuring them to see.

Polyhedra

Mathematicians have been puzzling over the properties of various solids for centuries. The group of solids most easy to study and categorize are called polyhedra (singular polyhedron).

Find any solid with flat surfaces. How many faces does it have? How many edges? How many corners?

This slice of cheese has 5 faces, 6 corners and 9 edges.

Corner

Face

Edge

Polyhedron is the Greek word for "many faced".

In the eighteenth century it was discovered that the answer to the sum faces + corners − edges was always 2.

Regular polyhedra

Although polyhedra come in all shapes and sizes, the existence of only five perfectly regular solids was proved more than 2000 years ago.

4 faces — Tetrahedron

6 faces — Cube

8 faces — Octahedron

Calculating volume

Just as it is difficult to visualize three-dimensional objects, it is hard to estimate how much space an object contains. Mathematics can help you to calculate the space accurately.

Which suitcase is bigger?

The amount of space an object occupies is its volume. For small solids, the volume is measured in cubic centimetres or cubic inches. One cubic centimetre is 1cm × 1cm × 1cm, or 1cm^3.

This cube represents 1cm^3.

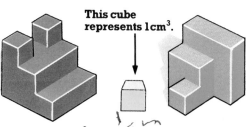

How many cm^3 do these two shapes contain?

This fishtank is a cuboid (a solid rectangle). You can work out its volume using the formula v = l × w × h (volume = length × width × height).

You would need 18 cubes to fill one layer of the tank which is 3 cubes wide and 6 cubes long.

You would need four layers to fill the fish tank so its volume is 4 × 18 cubes = 72 cubes.

Another way of putting this is that the volume is the area of the shape's base multiplied by its height. You can use this method to find out the volume of any shape which has the same cross-section throughout.

Can you work out a formula to find the volume of a cylinder?*

Building cubes

Six pairs of these polyhedra will build six cubes. Which one is left over?

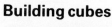

Each of these solids has every face the same shape, every edge the same length and every corner the same angle.

12 faces

Dodecahedron

20 faces

Icosahedron

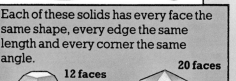

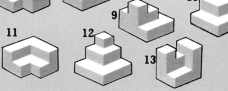

*Hint – area of a circle = πr^2

Angles

Most people think of an angle only as a corner between two straight lines. In fact, angles often describe turns, like those of a tree being felled or a key in a lock. You can measure the size of an angle, that is, how many degrees (written °) the turn is, by using a protractor or angle indicator.*

Right angles

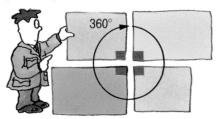

The corners of squares and rectangles are special angles called right angles. A full turn is 360° and four right angles make a complete turn. So a right angle is always 90°.

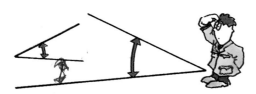

These angles are both 30°, so the length of the arms does not alter the amount of turn.

Angle names

A right angle is usually marked with a corner sign.

Angles which are less than 90° are acute.

Reflex angles are those which are more than 180°.

Obtuse angles are those between 90° and 180°.

Calculating angles without protractors

You can often work out the size of an angle by using logic rather than by measuring it. Logic enables you to arrive at theorems; a theorem is a mathematical rule which can be proved to be true. Below are some basic theorems involving angles.

1. Angles of a triangle

Tear off the corners of a triangle and place them together to make half a circle. This shows that the angles of a triangle together total 180°.

Because this is true for any triangle, many theorems of geometry are based upon this fact.

2. Angles inside polygons

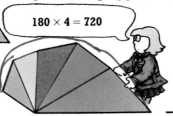

180 × 4 = 720

Because any polygon can be divided into a number of triangles, you can always calculate the total value of its angles. For example, a hexagon will make four triangles, so the angles in a hexagon must total 720°. How many degrees is each angle in a regular hexagon? **

3. Angles on a straight line

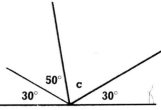

When angles fit together to make a straight line, you can imagine a half circle where they meet. So the sum of the angles on the line must be 180°.

This means that, if only one angle is unknown, it is possible to calculate it. Can you find the value of c?

*Go to page 37 to see how to use a protractor.
**Go to page 12 for more about regular shapes.

More angle theorems

Below, there are two more angle theorems. Because they refer to a number of angles, it is necessary to label the angles. An angle sign can be placed over the appropriate letter, for example, $\hat{B}$ or $\hat{E}$; or before the letter, e.g. $\lfloor B$ or $\lfloor E$.

In the picture on the right there are three angles meeting at D and you can define each one by showing the lines which form it.

A$\hat{D}$B, B$\hat{D}$A, A$\hat{D}$C and $\lfloor$CDA all describe the angle marked in red.

Alternate angles theorem

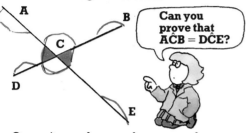

Can you prove that A$\hat{C}$B = D$\hat{C}$E?

Opposite angles are always equal.
Proof:
Where two lines cross, the four angles total 360°:

A$\hat{C}$D + A$\hat{C}$B = 180° because DCB is a straight line.
E$\hat{C}$B + A$\hat{C}$B = 180° because ACE is also a straight line.
So A$\hat{C}$D = E$\hat{C}$B.

Exterior angles theorem

Use the exterior angle theorem to prove that D$\hat{E}$G = $\hat{A}$ + $\hat{D}$.

An exterior angle (such as F$\hat{D}$E) is equal to the two opposite angles of the triangle ($\hat{A}$ and $\hat{E}$).
Proof:
$\hat{A}$ + $\hat{E}$ + A$\hat{D}$E = 180° because the three angles form a triangle.
F$\hat{D}$E + A$\hat{D}$E = 180° because they form the straight line ADF.
So $\hat{A}$ + $\hat{E}$ = F$\hat{D}$E.

Measuring in degrees

The first serious astronomers were the ancient Babylonians who believed that the year was made up of 12 moons each lasting 30 days and so there were 360 days in a year. It was perhaps for this reason that the circle was divided into 360 degrees. After 4000 years we still use these degrees to measure directions and angles.

Bearings and navigation

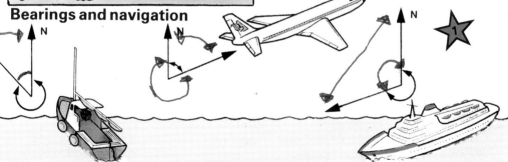

Ships and planes record their direction of travel using bearings. A bearing is the angle measured clockwise from north. The aeroplane, barge and cruiser are travelling on bearings of 68°, 317° and 251°. Which bearing relates to which craft?

Topology

Have you ever tried to draw an envelope without letting your pencil leave the paper and without retracing the lines? Can you copy the diagram on the right without tracing the same line twice?

There are many versions of these puzzles. It is possible to solve them mathematically by using the rules of topology. You can find out about these on these two pages.

The seven bridges of Königsberg

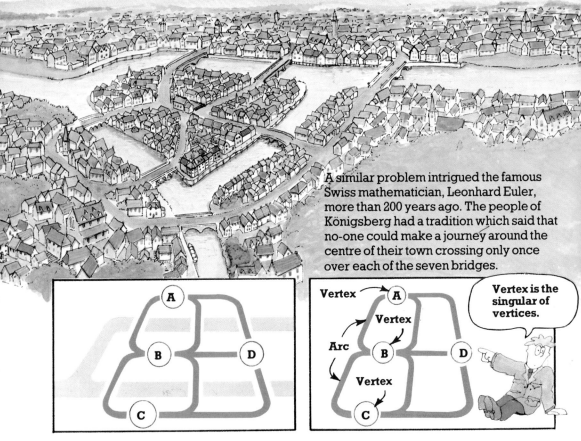

A similar problem intrigued the famous Swiss mathematician, Leonhard Euler, more than 200 years ago. The people of Königsberg had a tradition which said that no-one could make a journey around the centre of their town crossing only once over each of the seven bridges.

Vertex is the singular of vertices.

Euler drew a sketch map of the town, labelling the four separate parts A, B, C and D. He then marked each of the possible routes from one point to the next over the bridges, by tracing around the diagram with a pencil.

In doing this, he proved that it was not possible to cross every bridge just once. Euler called the diagram a network, the points vertices, and the lines arcs. If a network could be traced passing along all the arcs only once, he called it traversable.

Understanding networks

If all the vertices are even, or there are only one or two odd vertices, the figure can be traversed.

A figure cannot be traversed if it has more than two odd vertices.

← **Even vertex**

Odd vertex

While doing his research, Euler found that he did not need to draw a network to find out if it was traversable. He discovered that it depended upon how many odd or even vertices there were.

A vertex is called odd when it has an odd number of arcs meeting at one point, and it is called even when there are an even number of arcs meeting.

Topology in everyday life

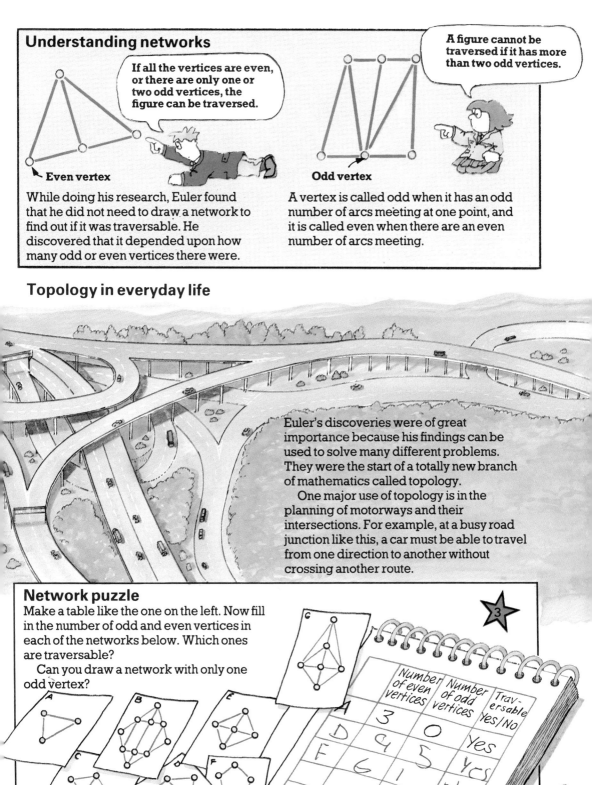

Euler's discoveries were of great importance because his findings can be used to solve many different problems. They were the start of a totally new branch of mathematics called topology.

One major use of topology is in the planning of motorways and their intersections. For example, at a busy road junction like this, a car must be able to travel from one direction to another without crossing another route.

Network puzzle

Make a table like the one on the left. Now fill in the number of odd and even vertices in each of the networks below. Which ones are traversable?

Can you draw a network with only one odd vertex?

	Number of even vertices	Number of odd vertices	Traversable Yes/No
	3	0	Yes
D	4	5	Yes
F	6	1	Yes
			No

23

Fractions

You're ³⁄₄hr late!

My bike got a puncture when I was half-way here.

²⁄₅ means 2 × ¹⁄₅.

We use fractions frequently in conversation without even realizing it. It is easy to picture the amount a fraction represents because it compares itself with 1.

This is ¹⁄₅ of the cake because 5 pieces like it make up the whole cake.

Sizing up fractions

There are two parts to a fraction, the numerator and denominator.

The larger the denominator, the smaller the pieces.

The numerator is the number of pieces.

The denominator shows the size of the pieces.

Which is bigger, ¹⁄₁₀ or ¹⁄₃?

²/₅

2/5:

|1 |2 |3

Percentages

Percentages are fractions of 100. See if you can work out the percentages in this story.

Astor has spent the week mending lunarbugs and has just been paid for his work. He goes into town to spend his money and his first stop is the bank.

Aries

20% off marked prices

240

BANK
Interest rate 10%

The bank will pay him an extra ¹⁰⁄₁₀₀ or ¹⁄₁₀ of the money he deposits with them.

To calculate the interest on 120 solars at the rate of 10% per year, he multiplies 120 by ¹⁰⁄₁₀₀.

1. How much interest will he have after one year?

2. How much money will he have in his account after 2 years?

Astor's next stop is Mr Aries' clothes shop. Mr Aries is offering a reduction of 20% – or ¹⁄₅ off (²⁰⁄₁₀₀ = ¹⁄₅).

To calculate the saving on this space suit, Astor multiplies 240 by ¹⁄₅.

3. How much will he save?

He could take the amount he saves away from 240 solars to obtain the price, but a quicker method would be to calculate 80% directly.

4. What is 240 × 80%?

Simplifying fractions

24/32 = 12/16 = 6/8 = 3/4

It is often convenient to change a fraction's denominator to make a calculation easier.

Adding fractions

To add fractions, first change each fraction to the same size sections, using the rules for simplifying fractions described above.

$\frac{1}{2}$ + $\frac{1}{3}$ = ?

$\frac{3}{6}$ + $\frac{2}{6}$ = $\frac{5}{6}$

Both ½ and ⅓ can be changed to sixths – remember to change the numerators too.

Subtracting fractions

$\frac{3}{4}$ − $\frac{3}{5}$ = ?

$\frac{15}{20} - \frac{12}{20}$ = $\frac{3}{20}$

These fractions can be changed to twentieths.

You can simplify a fraction by either multiplying or dividing both the numerator and denominator by the same number.

Half of a half

$$\frac{1}{2} \times \frac{1}{2} = \frac{1}{4}$$

You might expect that multiplying would always make a number bigger – but not if you are multiplying by a fraction.

$$20 \times \frac{1}{4} = \frac{20}{4}$$

$$\frac{20}{4} = 5$$

$$\frac{3}{8} \times \frac{2}{3} = \frac{6}{24}$$

$$\frac{6}{24} = \frac{1}{4}$$

To multiply fractions, first multiply the numerators and denominators, then simplify.

Astor now decides to treat himself to dinner. When the time comes to settle the bill, he has to pay for the food, plus a service charge of 10% for the waiter, and a 15% cover charge to the proprietor.

The two bills drawn up by the proprietor and the waiter result in the same amount of money being owed by Astor.

The waiter would like to have the service charge added last, but the owner insists that the cover charge is the last to be added. You can see why!

BILL

26.00
+ cover 15%   3.90
              29.90
+ service 10% 2.99
              32.89
TOTAL

BILL

26.00
+ service 10% 2.60
              28.60
+ cover 15%   4.29
TOTAL   32.89

Ratios

Ratios are to do with proportions. For example, if you make a jug of orange juice with two cups of concentrated orange and five cups of water, you are mixing the ingredients in the ratio of two to five (written 2:5). You can increase or decrease all the ingredients as long as the proportions stay the same.

You could make two jugs with four cups of orange and ten cups of water . . .

. . . or half a jug with one cup of orange and two and a half cups of water.

Working out ratios

1. Calculate the total number of shares.

2. Find the value of each share.

3. Find out how much each person gets.

There are 10 shares (5 + 3 + 2).

Each share is 180 ÷ 10 = 18 pieces.

Roy gets 5 × 18 = 90 pieces, Alison gets 3 × 18 = 54 pieces, I get 2 × 18 = 36 pieces.

Alison, Roy and Harry have just robbed the safe of a large bank and are trying to divide up the loot (180 pieces of gold) fairly. Since Roy is the leader, he wants a larger share than Alison or Harry.

Alison thinks that as Harry was only the look-out man, she should get more than him. They finally decide to share it out in the ratio of 5:3:2. To do this they have to follow the three steps displayed above.

Comparing ratios

Which material contains the most wool?

You may find it easier to compare these two ratios if you write the ratio 55:45 in the simpler form of 11:9.

VIYELLA
55% wool
45% cotton

CLYDELLA.
2 parts wool
8 parts cotton

This tells you that the Viyella material contains 11 parts wool out of 20 parts in total. The Clydella material contains 4 out of 20 parts wool, so Viyella has more wool in it.

This map uses a scale of 1:25 000 which means that 1cm (or 1 inch) on the map represents 25 000cm (or 25 000 inches) on the ground. What would 1m on the same map represent?

Ratios are also used by bookmakers. You pay one token to bet on the horse Joyful, and if he wins you win five tokens. What would you win if you bet one token on Terror?

Horse Odd.
Royal 9-1
Terror 100-8
Joyful 5-1

Ratios and volumes

A toy car is built in the ratio of 1:20 to a life-size car. But 20 toy cars would not even fill the boot of a real car, let alone equal it in size. Why?

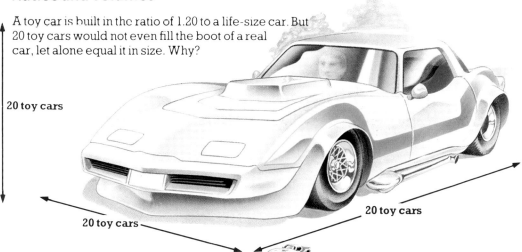

20 toy cars

20 toy cars

20 toy cars

The answer is that the ratio of 1:20 gives a comparison of *each* length of the two cars. The toy car is ½₀th as long as the real one, ½₀th as wide and ½₀th as high.

You would need 20 × 20 × 20 toy cars to fill up the same space as a real car. So in fact, the ratio of the volumes of the two cars is 1:8000.

Puzzles

Bottle A holds 1 litre of wine and bottle B holds 2 litres. Why isn't bottle B twice the height of bottle A?

If it takes 50 biscuits to fill this jar, would a jar identical in shape but twice the size be filled by 100 biscuits?

Triangle ratios

Ancient Egyptians measured out the base of a pyramid with a rope which had 12 equal sections knotted on it. This was held taut in the shape of a triangle with sides in the ratio of 3:4:5. The angle opposite the longest side was always a right angle. Probably the most well-known theorem in mathematics, Pythagoras' theorem explains why.

Pythagoras' theorem

Pythagoras was a famous Greek mathematician. He discovered that when a triangle has a right angle and its three sides are, say, a, b and c, then $c^2 = a^2 + b^2$.

6 : 12 : 13   9 : 12 : 15   7 : 8 : 10

Above are the ratios of the sides of three different triangles. Only one of them has a right angle – which one? Use Pythagoras' theorem to find out.

Sets

Many different areas of mathematics involve organizing numbers and shapes into sets. Mathematicians have made it easier to study these sets by inventing the special symbols listed below.

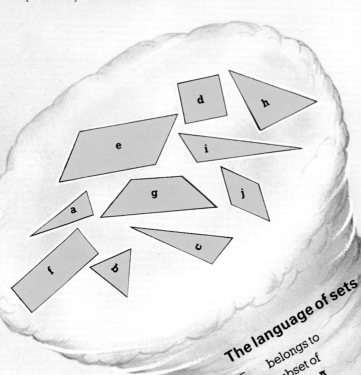

These shapes can be arranged into many different sets, such as the set of triangles, the set of quadrilaterals, the set of polygons with equal sides, and polygons with right angles. Yet they are all members of the set of polygons which we can call **P**.

If **A** is the set of those shapes with equal sides, then **A** = {**b,d,j**}.

If **B** is the set of those shapes with a right angle, then **B** = {**a,d,f,h**}.

The language of sets

∈	belongs to
⊂	subset of
A	the set **A**
A'	the set of members not in **A**
∅	empty set
∩	intersection (and)
∪	union (or)
n	number of members in

Can you identify the sets **C** and **D** when **C** = {**a,b,c,h,i**} and **D** = {**d,e,f,g,j**}?

C⊂**P** means that the set **C** is a sub-set of the larger set **P**.

b∈**C** means that **b** is a member of **C**. If **b**∈**C**, then **b**∈**P** because **C** is a subset of **P**.

The symbol **n** is used to show how many members a group has.

What is **n(A∩B)**?
What about **n(A∪B)**?

{circle, square, hexagon, cube, rhombus

Odd one out

What could be the odd one out in this set?

Venn diagrams

In the diagram on the opposite page, some of the sets overlap because a shape such as **d** belongs in sets **A**, **B** and **D**. In 1880, John Venn developed a simple device to show relationships between various sets, called a Venn diagram.

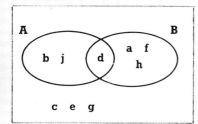

No member occurs twice.

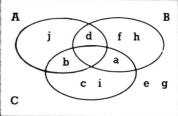

This Venn diagram shows sets **A** and **B**. The overlap is **A ∩ B** and so **d ∈ A ∩ B**. Any element which is not a member of **A** or **B** is placed outside the loops.

This is a Venn diagram for sets **A**, **B** and **C**. The overlap of all three is **A ∩ B ∩ C**. The shape **a** has moved to be inside **B** and **C** but not in **A**, so **a ∈ A′ ∩ B ∩ C**. What set is **A ∩ B ∩ C**?

Matrices

	NY	L	P	M	D	HK
NY	0	2	1	0	0	0
L	2	0	1	1	1	0
P	1	1	0	0	1	0
M	0	1	0	0	1	1
D	0	1	1	1	0	1
HK	0	0	0	1	1	0

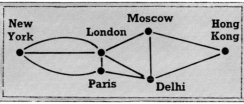

Some information about sets of numbers is more easily stored in a matrix than in a list or Venn diagram.

The matrix above shows the number of direct flights between certain airports. While you can read the map just as easily for this small number of air routes, for a large amount of information a matrix is very useful.

Journey puzzle

Mrs Martin wants to travel from Hong Kong to New York but there are no direct flights. An airport official suggests a route she might take. Can you translate it?

HK ∩ D ∩ {L ∪ P} ∩ NY

Beyond numbers

Set Z is the set of counting numbers. It contains an infinite number of numbers which we can show by saying $n(Z) = \infty$.

Set T also contains an infinite number of numbers so $n(T) = \infty$. But T does not contain the first nine numbers so it looks as if $\infty - 9 = \infty$.

This seems impossible to us unless we can accept the fact that we have argued correctly. The rules for numbers which describe the size of infinite sets seem to follow a different logic from ordinary numbers. It is an area that modern mathematics is still exploring . . .

29

Statistics

Statistics is a new branch of maths developed to record information and to help predict likely events. Statisticians obtain their information by collecting data, for example, by questioning a number of people who are representative of the population they want to test. This is called "sampling". Their findings can be presented in a number of ways, as shown below.

Researching a holiday resort

Lindsay works for a tour operator and is doing a survey on a holiday resort. She asks a sample of holiday makers various questions, such as "What nationality are you?", and "How did you travel to the resort?". She then displays her results in the five different forms shown below.

1. Pie chart

What is the most common nationality among the holidaymakers?

The circle below is divided up into sections which correspond to the percentage of each nationality.

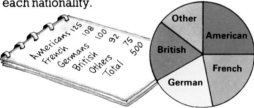

To calculate the angle for each section she finds out what fraction each nationality is of the total number of people. There are $^{125}/_{500}$ ($\frac{1}{4}$) Americans, so their angle is $\frac{1}{4} \times 360° = 90°$. Can you calculate the other angles?

2. Block diagram

What method of transport did most people use to get to the resort?

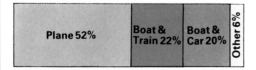

This information is displayed in a block diagram. For a block diagram, a rectangle is divided up in the same way as the circle was divided up for the pie chart.

3. Histogram

How many people stayed at the Hotel Cana in the years 1978-84?

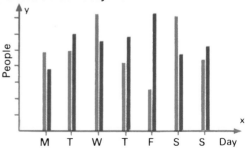

Each column of this histogram represents the number of people for that year; it is not related to any other year.

4. Frequency graph

How many people visited the beach in the first two weeks of June?

The advantage of this graph is that you can show a number of weeks on the same graph. Can you guess on which days it rained and on which days it was very hot?

30

Data compiled by statisticians is used by governments for long term planning, and by market researchers before launching a new product.

Three kinds of average

We often need to gain a quick understanding of the *general* size of a group of figures. Statisticians use one of three averages, the mode, median and mean, depending on the task.

The average size is 6.

Fred needs to know the average size of people's feet so that he can stock more sandals in that size. His kind of average is the mode: the most popular size.

In this game, the player must hit a weight with a hammer. If his hit is above average in strength, a bell rings. The maker of the game found the average strength by recording the scores of 100 people and finding the median. The median is the middle score.

5. Scatter graph

Is there a relationship between the amount of money spent and the age of the spenders?
A scatter graph is used to plot information which seems unconnected, to see whether any trends appear.

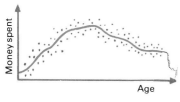

Here Lindsay plots the amount of money spent in a week against the age of the spender. What does the graph show?

The average most widely used is the mean. This is found by totalling all the items in the groups and dividing the total by the number of groups. Here the total number of crabs caught was 21. If they were shared out equally, each friend would get 7; so the mean caught was 7.

What are the mean, mode and median number of people who go swimming during this week?

Statistics don't lie ... but liars use statistics!

Look carefully at advertising or political statements which use statistics, as they can be misleading.

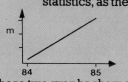

These two graphs show exactly the same information but the one on the right has been scaled to show a rise in the birth rate. Can you see how this has been achieved?

Monday 380
Tuesday 415
Wednesday 380
Thursday 340
Friday 210
Saturday 300
Sunday 365

Graphs

Have you ever stopped to consider the relationship between the size of a bag of sugar and its weight? The larger the bag of sugar, the heavier it is. There are many different quantities which are related to one another in a similar way, such as the distance a car travels and its speed, or the age and height of a tree. The French mathematician, René Descartes (1596-1650) invented the co-ordinate system to illustrate such relationships on graphs.

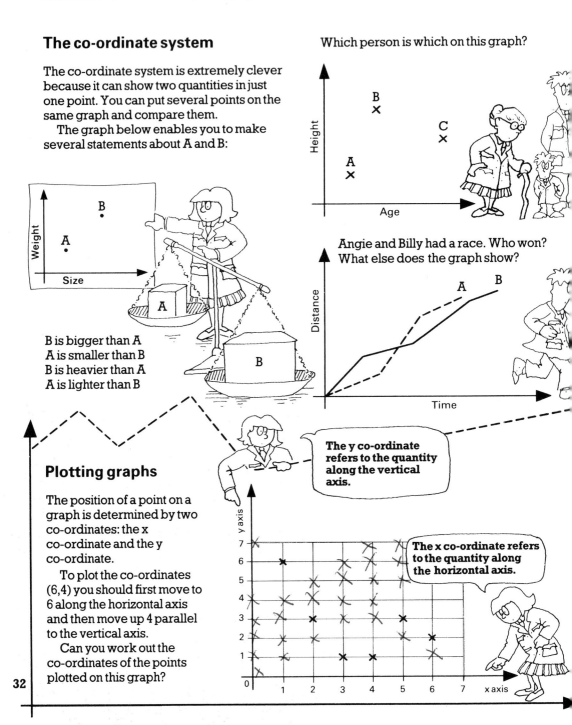

The co-ordinate system

The co-ordinate system is extremely clever because it can show two quantities in just one point. You can put several points on the same graph and compare them.

The graph below enables you to make several statements about A and B:

B is bigger than A
A is smaller than B
B is heavier than A
A is lighter than B

Which person is which on this graph?

Angie and Billy had a race. Who won? What else does the graph show?

The y co-ordinate refers to the quantity along the vertical axis.

Plotting graphs

The position of a point on a graph is determined by two co-ordinates: the x co-ordinate and the y co-ordinate.

To plot the co-ordinates (6,4) you should first move to 6 along the horizontal axis and then move up 4 parallel to the vertical axis.

Can you work out the co-ordinates of the points plotted on this graph?

The x co-ordinate refers to the quantity along the horizontal axis.

Picture puzzle

The pictures below tell the story of a hiker's journey. The graph on the right also shows her journey with each dot representing the distance travelled by the walker at a given time. Can you fill in the missing information in the pictures?

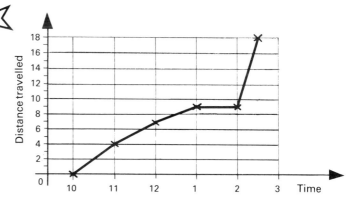

Reading graphs

The most important part of reading a graph is to notice what the axes are showing.

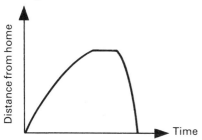

This graph shows the same journey as the graphs above, but the axes are labelled differently. Instead of showing the distance travelled in total, this graph indicates the distance the walker is from her starting point.

Warning

Don't jump to conclusions!

A graph may seem to indicate that, for example, people score more highly on a maths test as the shoe size gets bigger. Does that mean that the bigger your feet, the better you are at mathematics?

Always watch out for additional factors which may be causing the relationship.

33

More about graphs

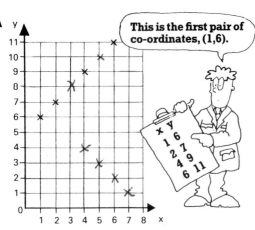

This is the first pair of co-ordinates, (1,6).

x	y
1	6
2	7
4	9
6	11

Look at the two sets of numbers on the pad above. Each number on the right is five more than the number on its left. The pairs of numbers are plotted on the graph above.

Because each pair of numbers has the same relationship (the y number is always five more than the x number), all the points lie on a straight line. Any other pair which has this relationship will also fit on the line, for example, ⁻2,3 and 2½,7½.

Describing relationships

You can write $y = x + 5$ to say that all the y numbers are five more than the x numbers. The line of dots on the graph is called the $y = x + 5$ line.

Another way of putting this is $x \rightarrow x + 5$. This is usually read as "x maps to x plus five". You can use whichever you find easier.

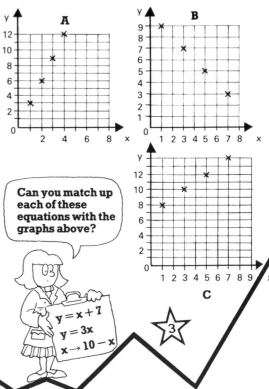

Can you match up each of these equations with the graphs above?

$y = x + 7$

$y = 3x$

$x \rightarrow 10 - x$

Solving equations

Each of the equations shown above describes a relationship which is true for many pairs of numbers. You could always find the value of y if you knew the value of x, and vice-versa.

On page 21 (Angles), you saw that $110 + c = 180$. Because the total value of the angles was 180°, you could find the value of c.

Another way to find c is to plot the graph for the equation $d = c + 110$.* You can then find the value of c when d is 180.

This method can be very time-consuming, and there are other ways of solving equations. On the opposite page are two different ways of solving these equations:

$2y - 7 = 11$ and $\dfrac{5(F - 32)}{9} = 20$.

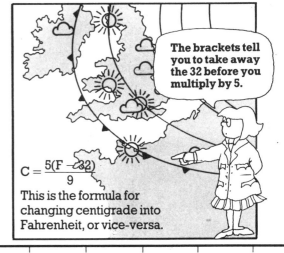

The brackets tell you to take away the 32 before you multiply by 5.

$$C = \frac{5(F - 32)}{9}$$

This is the formula for changing centigrade into Fahrenheit, or vice-versa.

*You can use any letters you like to represent quantities in an equation.

Plotting equations

You can plot any relationship which is presented in either of the two forms described earlier. Follow the steps on the right to plot the graph $y = x + 3$.

1) Work out some number pairs which have this relationship:

x y
(1,4)
(3,6)
(5,8)

2) Plot the numbers on a graph.
3) Join up the points.

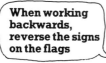

When working backwards, reverse the signs on the flags

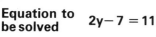

Equation to be solved $2y - 7 = 11$

Equation to be solved $\dfrac{5(F - 32)}{9} = 20$

Function method

Explanation

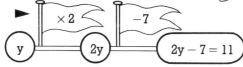

A value for y is doubled, then 7 is taken away from it. The answer is 11.

Solution

To find out what value of y produces the answer 11, work backwards:

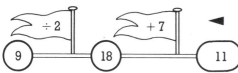

Answer: $y = 9$

Algebra method

Explanation

7 must be taken away from 2y to make the value 11.

Solution

If $2y - 7 = 11$
then $2y = 11 + 7$
so $2y = 18$
and $y = 9$.

Answer: $y = 9$

The word algebra comes from the title of a book written in about 830 AD. In this book the famous Arab mathematician Mohamed Al-Khowarizmi describes his method of *al-jabr* to solve equations.

Function method

Explanation

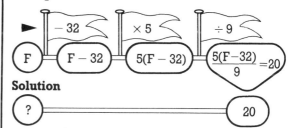

Solution

Again, you should work backwards:

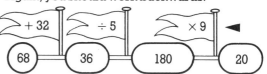

Answer: $F = 68$ so when the temperature is 20°C, it is 68°F.

Algebra method

Explanation

32 is taken away from F, and the number left is multiplied by 5, then divided by 9. The value after doing this is 20.

Solution

If $\dfrac{5(F - 32)}{9} = 20$

then $5(F - 32) = 20 \times 9$
so $5(F - 32) = 180$
and $F - 32 = \dfrac{180}{5} = 36$

If $F - 32 = 36$
then $F = 36 + 32 = 68$
Answer: $F = 68$

Geometry

Geometry is to do with drawing accurate mathematical diagrams. Methods were being studied in Egypt as early as the 14th century BC when people paid their taxes according to the size of their land. Hence its name which comes from the Greek word *geo* (earth) and *metron* (measure). Today, map-making, surveying, aircraft design, architecture and computer circuitry all depend upon geometric precision. Below are some standard geometric constructions.

Make sure you have all the necessary equipment before you start.

Drawing a line of exact length

First draw a line longer than you want and make a mark near one end.

Then open your compasses to the length you need.

Place the compass point on the mark on the line and draw a light arc across the line with the pencil.

Drawing a triangle (sides 5cm, 3cm and 7cm)

1. Mark off a length of 7cm on a straight line.

2. Open the compasses to 3cm, place the point on one end of the line and draw an arc, as shown above.

3. Open the compasses to 5cm and draw a second arc from the other end of the line.

4. Join the three corners and check the measurements of the sides.

Greek mathematics today

Even today, the ancient Greeks are admired for the precision of their geometry. One of the most famous Greek mathematicians was Euclid. His painstakingly accurate diagrams enabled him to make some very surprising discoveries, two of which are described on the right.

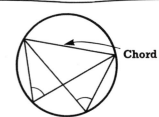

Chord

When a chord is drawn across a circle, any angle drawn from it to the edge of the circle will always be the same size, provided that the points are on the same side of the chord.

Bisecting a line

To bisect means to cut in half.

1. Open the compasses to more than half the length of the line.

A   B

2. From one end of the line, draw an arc above and below the line.

3. Now do the same from the other end, without changing the compasses.

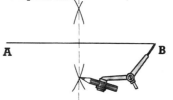

A   B

4. Join the two crosses and this line will cut AB exactly in half.

Bisecting an angle

1. Place the compass on each arc in turn, and draw two new arcs which cross each other, as shown below.

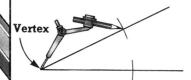

Vertex

2. Place the compass on each arc in turn, and draw two new arcs which cross each other, as shown below.

3. A line drawn from the angle to where the arcs cross will cut the angle in half.

Drawing parallel lines (2cm apart)

1. Draw a line about 4cm long.

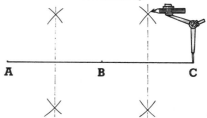

A   B   C

2. Mark three points, A, B and C. Bisect AB and bisect BC.

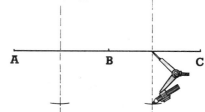

A   B   C

3. Mark off 2cm on each line. Join the two points where the arcs cross the lines.

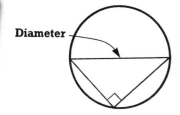

Diameter

When a chord goes through the centre of the circle (its diameter), any angle which you draw from its ends will be 90°, no matter where the point comes on the circle.

The easiest way to test these theorems is to draw some circles and chords, then measure the angles with a protractor.

3. Read off the size of the angle on the other arm. Is this 100° or 80°?

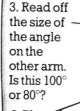

2. Place the centre of the protractor on the vertex of the angle.

1. Line up the zero line with one arm of the angle.

Number patterns

Since the time of Pythagoras (550 BC) mathematicians have made many of their discoveries by studying the patterns which occur in our number system. You can find out about a few of these patterns on these two pages.

Squares

The small figure ^{2} above any number tells you to multiply that number by itself.

$$2^2 = 4 \qquad 9^2 = 81 \qquad 12^2 = 144$$

The power 2 is usually called "square" because the multiplication can be illustrated by a square:

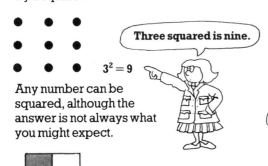

Three squared is nine.

$$3^2 = 9$$

Any number can be squared, although the answer is not always what you might expect.

$$\tfrac{1}{2}^2 = \tfrac{1}{4}$$

Square roots

The square root of a number is the number which, when multiplied by itself, will give the original number.

The square root of 12.96 is 3.6 because 3.6 × 3.6 is 12.96.

Powers

Many calculations in mathematics involve multiplying numbers by themselves and it is quite common to meet powers greater than 2. 1 million is

Another word for powers is indices.

What is 2^3?

$$10 \times 10 \times 10 \times 10 \times 10 \times 10 = 10^6$$

The power of 6 indicates that 6 tens are multiplied together. $2^5 = 32$ because 2^5 means $2 \times 2 \times 2 \times 2 \times 2$. The power of 3 is usually called cube.

Prime numbers

Prime numbers have intrigued mathematicians for centuries because they refuse to fit into any kind of recognizable pattern. A prime number has no factors except 1 and itself. A factor of a number will divide into that number exactly.

The number 40 is not a prime because it can be divided exactly by 1, 2, 4, 5, 8, 10, 20 and 40 so it has eight factors. But 41 is only divisible by 1 and itself so it must be a prime.

Spotting prime numbers

One way of finding the prime numbers under 121 is to divide every number by 2, 3, 5 and 7. If a number can be divided exactly, it is rejected. If the number cannot be divided exactly by 2, 3, 5 or 7 then it must be a prime.

If the test were extended to include dividing numbers by 11, it would find all the prime numbers under 169. Can you see why this should be?

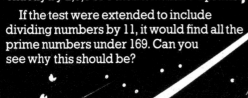

Multiplying with powers

$$2^5 \times 2^3 = (2 \times 2 \times 2 \times 2 \times 2) \times (2 \times 2 \times 2)$$
$$= 2^8$$

When multiplying identical numbers with the same, or different powers, you need only add the powers.

What is $2^7 \times 2^2$?

Dividing with powers

$$2^5 \div 2^3 = \frac{2 \times 2 \times 2 \times 2 \times 2}{2 \times 2 \times 2} = 2^2$$

When dividing the same number with different powers, just subtract the indices.

$$2^3 \div 2^5 = \frac{2 \times 2 \times 2}{2 \times 2 \times 2 \times 2 \times 2} = 2^{-2} \text{ or } \frac{1}{2^2}$$

A negative power will always tell you that the number is a reciprocal. A reciprocal is a fraction where the top part is 1.

$$10^{-3} = \frac{1}{10^3} = \frac{1}{1000}$$

Can you write 10^{-5} in reciprocal form?

Standard form

Scientists frequently have to deal with very large numbers and very small numbers. For example, the distance from Earth to the nearest star, Alpha Centauri, is about 40 350 000 000 000 000 meters. The wavelength of sodium street lights is 0.000 000 589 meters. Because it is inconvenient to write numbers like this – they are hard to visualize and it is easy to make mistakes – they can be written in standard form.

Standard form is always a number between one and ten, multiplied by a power of ten. Because 40 350 000 000 000 000 is the same as 4.035 × 10 000 000 000 000 000 it can be written as 4.035×10^{16}. Similarly, the wavelength of sodium light can be written as 5.89×10^{-7}.

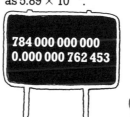

784 000 000 000
0.000 000 762 453

Can you write these numbers in standard form?

Formulae for primes

Many mathematicians have attempted to write formulae which would find prime numbers.

n^2	$-$	n	$+$	41	$=$	p
Any number multiplied by itself.		Subtract the original number.		Add 41		The total is a prime number.

Although this formula works for some values of n, it fails when n is 41. Try the formula out and see for yourself.

÷3

÷7

Primes under 121

Secret codes

No rules can be found to spot the large numbers which are primes; they can only be found by lengthy divisions. The most recently found prime number contains 25 692 digits and it took several weeks of computer time to produce it. Because prime numbers are so elusive, they are used in the most modern secret codes. It is the only use so far found for primes.

Binary numbers

Although computers and electronic calculators can cope with incredibly complex problems, they are unable to handle our decimal number system directly. They handle information in the form of patterns of electrical signals. Each signal can either be ON or OFF. Because of this, their number system is written using only two symbols: 1 (representing ON) and 0 (OFF). This is called the base two or binary system.

How binary works

The base two system works just like decimals (which is also called the base ten system). Each digit has a different value depending on its position in the total number. In the decimal system, the digits show the number of 1s, 10s, 100s, 1000s, etc. (see page 6). In the binary system, the digits show the number of 1s, 2s, 4s, 8s, etc.

So $23_{base\ ten}$ is written $10111_{base\ two}$.

Example: $23_{base\ ten}$ in binary:

16s	8s	4s	2s	1s
1	0	1	1	1
1×16	0×8	1×4	1×2	1×1

$16 + 4 + 2 + 1 = 23$

In binary you can write *any* number using just 1 and 0. To obtain the next column heading, just double the number which heads the column before it. Each column heading is, in fact, a power of two, and in decimals, each is a power of ten.*

To translate $37_{base\ ten}$, for example, to binary, you need to work out how many 32s, 16s, 8s, 4s, 2s and 1s it contains. How would you write it in binary?

Translating binary

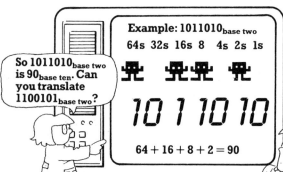

Example: $1011010_{base\ two}$

64s	32s	16s	8	4s	2s	1s
1	0	1	1	0	1	0

$64 + 16 + 8 + 2 = 90$

So $1011010_{base\ two}$ is $90_{base\ ten}$. Can you translate $1100101_{base\ two}$?

One less puzzle

Can you find the total of $1 + 2 + 3 + 8 + 16 + 32 + 64$ without doing any addition?

$1 + 2 = 3$
$1 + 2 + 4 = 7$
$1 + 2 + 4 + 8 = 15$
$1 + 2 + 4 + 8 + 16 = 31$
$1 + 2 + 4 + 8 + 16 + 32 = 63$

When you want to convert any number from binary to decimal, write the column headings above each digit starting on the right, and add the columns which have a figure 1.

40

Binary sums

It is possible to calculate in binary without translating the numbers into decimals.

The sum $1101_{\text{base two}}$ plus $101_{\text{base two}}$ is shown in separate stages below.

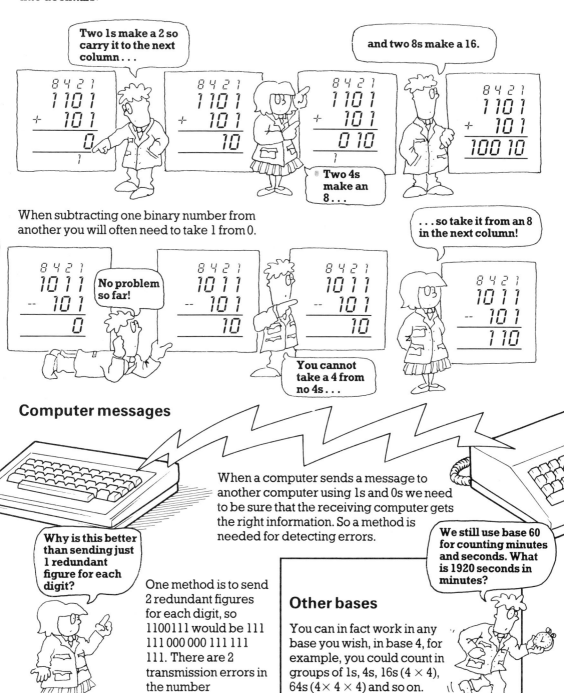

Two 1s make a 2 so carry it to the next column . . .

and two 8s make a 16.

$$
\begin{array}{r}
8\ 4\ 2\ 1 \\
1\ 1\ 0\ 1 \\
+\quad 1\ 0\ 1 \\
\hline
0
\end{array}
$$

$$
\begin{array}{r}
8\ 4\ 2\ 1 \\
1\ 1\ 0\ 1 \\
+\quad 1\ 0\ 1 \\
\hline
1\ 0
\end{array}
$$

$$
\begin{array}{r}
8\ 4\ 2\ 1 \\
1\ 1\ 0\ 1 \\
+\quad 1\ 0\ 1 \\
\hline
0\ 1\ 0
\end{array}
$$

$$
\begin{array}{r}
8\ 4\ 2\ 1 \\
1\ 1\ 0\ 1 \\
+\quad 1\ 0\ 1 \\
\hline
1\ 0\ 0\ 1\ 0
\end{array}
$$

Two 4s make an 8 . . .

When subtracting one binary number from another you will often need to take 1 from 0.

. . . so take it from an 8 in the next column!

$$
\begin{array}{r}
8\ 4\ 2\ 1 \\
1\ 0\ 1\ 1 \\
-\quad 1\ 0\ 1 \\
\hline
0
\end{array}
$$

No problem so far!

$$
\begin{array}{r}
8\ 4\ 2\ 1 \\
1\ 0\ 1\ 1 \\
-\quad 1\ 0\ 1 \\
\hline
1\ 0
\end{array}
$$

$$
\begin{array}{r}
8\ 4\ 2\ 1 \\
1\ 0\ 1\ 1 \\
-\quad 1\ 0\ 1 \\
\hline
1\ 0
\end{array}
$$

You cannot take a 4 from no 4s . . .

$$
\begin{array}{r}
8\ 4\ 2\ 1 \\
1\ 0\ 1\ 1 \\
-\quad 1\ 0\ 1 \\
\hline
1\ 1\ 0
\end{array}
$$

Computer messages

When a computer sends a message to another computer using 1s and 0s we need to be sure that the receiving computer gets the right information. So a method is needed for detecting errors.

Why is this better than sending just 1 redundant figure for each digit?

One method is to send 2 redundant figures for each digit, so 1100111 would be 111 111 000 000 111 111 111. There are 2 transmission errors in the number 10100001011110000. Can you say what they are?

Other bases

You can in fact work in any base you wish, in base 4, for example, you could count in groups of 1s, 4s, 16s (4×4), 64s $(4 \times 4 \times 4)$ and so on.

We still use base 60 for counting minutes and seconds. What is 1920 seconds in minutes?

Probability

The study of probability is a very exciting branch of maths because it allows us to gain some insight into the future. Although they cannot predict exactly what will happen, the laws of probability indicate what event is most likely to occur. The next three pages explain how to work out probabilities. On page 45 there are some programs to use on a home computer to find out how accurate the forecasts are.

Toss a coin in the air. It is equally likely that it will land Heads or Tails. So the chance of a coin coming up Heads is 50-50 or ½.

Dice Doubles

Many games involve throwing two dice. What is the probability of scoring a double?

To calculate the probability of something happening, first find out all the possible outcomes.

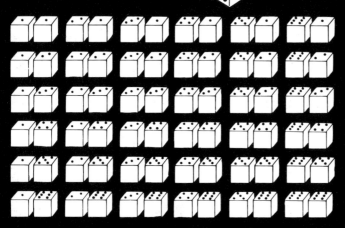

a) There are 36 possible ways in which the dice can land, all equally likely to happen.

b) Six of these possibilities are doubles so the probability of scoring a double is 6 out of 36 (or 1/6).

Go to page 45 to check the accuracy of these forecasts

Double doubles

What's the chance of throwing two doubles in a row?

Each time you throw a double with this first pair of dice, there is a one in six chance of throwing a double with the second pair. So there is a 1/6 × 1/6 (1/36) chance of throwing two doubles in a row.

Rule 1

When the outcome depends upon a series of events happening, multiply the separate probabilities.

Tree diagrams

For two children in a family to be boys, the probability is 1/4. This is because there are four possible arrangements for two children as this tree diagram shows, and a boy or girl are equally likely.

A tree diagram is a useful tool in probability because it enables all the possible arrangements to be found.

2 Boys   **Boy and Girl**   **Girl and Boy**   **2 Girls**

Winning chances

Use either of the methods below to work out your chances of winning at this game.

a) There are 52 playing cards which include 4 aces and 12 picture cards, i.e. 16 winning cards out of 52. The probability of winning is 16/52 = 4/13.

b) There are 4 aces, that's a probability of 4/52 (or 1/13) and 12 picture cards, another probability of 12/52 (3/13). That's a total probability of 1/13 + 3/13 = 4/13.

> Pick an ace or a picture card to win.

Probability scale

Mathematicians use a scale of 0 to 1 to show the likelihood of an event. They often rely on statistics to judge whether an event is likely or not.

1 – It will rain next year. (Statistics show it has rained every year so far.)

½ – Chance of randomly picking a left shoe out of a pair.

1/7 – Your birthday is on a Sunday.

0 – Astronauts will land on the sun.

1
½
1/7
0

1 means that it is as certain as can be that something will happen, and 0 means that an event is so unlikely as to be thought impossible.

Rule 2

For mutually exclusive events, that is when an event is not dependant on any other, add the probabilities.

Bingo

In this Bingo game ten numbers have been called. What is the probability of making a complete line at the next call?

After ten numbers there are still another eighty-nine possible numbers for the next call. This player can complete a line if 25 or 33 are called. The probability of winning is therefore 2/89.

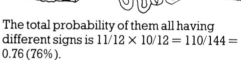

Matching birth signs

Did you know that in a group of three people there is a probability of 24/100 (24%) that two have been born under the same birth sign?

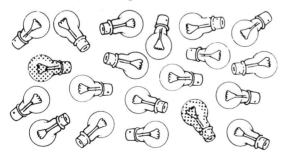

So the chance of two of us having the same birth sign is about 1/4 on the probability scale.

5

Can you see why you have to multiply the separate probabilities? Hint: see Rule 1.

Happy Birthday Niki
MARCH 4th

Happy Birthday Fiona
July 9th

Happy Birthday Alan
MARCH 12th

You first need to work out the chances of them having different birth signs. Niki's sign is Pisces, and as there are 12 signs in all, there is a 11/12 chance that Fiona's sign is not Pisces. If they are different, there is a 10/12 chance that Alan will not match either of their signs.

The total probability of them all having different signs is $11/12 \times 10/12 = 110/144 = 0.76$ (76%).

Quality Control

In a factory, thousands of lightbulbs are made each day. It is impossible to check each one, so a sample is taken.

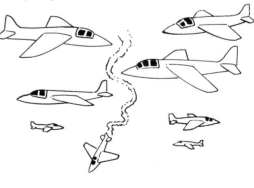

If one in ten of the sample lightbulbs are faulty, it is assumed that one in ten of all bulbs are likely to be faulty.

Although the probability of an error of 1 in 1000 may be acceptable in the case of lightbulbs, it would be disastrous as a gauge for aircraft as people's lives are at stake.

Computer programs

These programs will work on the Commodore 64, VIC 20, Apple, TRS-80 Colour Computer,* BBC, Electron and Spectrum. Lines marked ★ may need converting for the different computers. The conversions are listed at the bottom of the page. Run the programs and follow the instructions on the screen.

1. Prime number program

This program works out whether or not a number is a prime. You can use it to test out the systems on pages 38-39.

```
10 PRINT:PRINT "WHAT IS YOUR NUMBER"
20 LET F=0
30 INPUT N:IF N<3 THEN GOTO 70
40 FOR I=2 TO INT(N/2)
50 IF INT(N/I)=N/I THEN LET F=1:LET I=N-1
60 NEXT I
70 PRINT:PRINT N;" IS ";
80 IF F=1 THEN PRINT "NOT ";
90 PRINT "A PRIME NUMBER":GOTO 10
```

2. Dice program

This program makes the computer throw the equivalent of 36 pairs of dice and display the numbers on the screen. It provides a quick way to test the average number of doubles (see page 42).

```
★10 CLS
 20 PRINT:PRINT
 30 FOR I=1 TO 9
 40 FOR J=1 TO 4
★50 LET N1=INT(RND(1)*6+1)
★60 LET N2=INT(RND(1)*6+1)
★70 PRINT " ";N1;",";N2;
 80 IF N1=N2 THEN PRINT "*";
 90 IF N1<>N2 THEN PRINT " ";
100 NEXT J
110 PRINT:NEXT I:PRINT
120 PRINT "PRESS RETURN TO CONTINUE"
130 INPUT X$:GOTO 10
```

3. Fruit machine program

When you run this program, it asks you how many turns, or spins, you want. For each spin the names of three symbols come up in a row. Three identical symbols win a prize.

In each column of the fruit machine there are 10 cherries, 10 oranges, 6 lemons, 4 grapes, 2 melons and 1 bell. You can work out the probability of any combination being displayed using the methods on pages 42-44. The computer records how many times you win each prize. See if this relates to your probability forecasts.

```
 10 GOSUB 170:GOSUB 180
 20 PRINT "HOW MANY SPINS":INPUT NS
 30 FOR I=1 TO NS:FOR J=1 TO 3
★40 LET F=INT(RND(1)*33+1)
★50 LET X(J)=VAL(MID$(W$,F,1))
 60 NEXT J
 70 GOSUB 170:PRINT "SPINS : ";I
 80 PRINT:FOR J=1 TO 3
 90 PRINT F$(X(J));" ";:NEXT J:PRINT
100 IF X(1)=X(2) AND X(2)=X(3) THEN LET
     N(X(1))=N(X(1))+1:PRINT "* PRIZE *"
110 PRINT:PRINT "PRESS RETURN":INPUT X$
120 NEXT I
130 GOSUB 170:PRINT "TOTAL SPINS = ";NS
140 PRINT:FOR I=1 TO 6
150 PRINT "3  X  ";F$(I);TAB(18);N(I)
160 NEXT I:PRINT:STOP
★170 CLS:PRINT:PRINT:RETURN
★180 DIM F$(6):DIM N(6):DIM X(3)
190 FOR I=1 TO 6:READ F$(I):NEXT I
200 LET W$="11111111112222222222233333334444556"
210 RETURN
220 DATA "CHERRY","ORANGE","LEMON"
230 DATA "GRAPE","MELON","BELL"
```

Dice program conversions

Commodore 64:
```
10 PRINT CHR$(147)
```

VIC 20:
```
70 PRINT N1;CHR$(157);N2;CHR$(157);
```

Apple:
```
10 HOME
```

Spectrum:
```
50,60 Replace RND(1) with RND
```

TRS-80:
```
50,60 Replace RND(1) with RND(0)
70 PRINT N1;CHR$(8);N2;
```

Fruit machine conversions

Commodore 64 and VIC 20:
```
170 PRINT CHR$(147):PRINT:PRINT:RETURN
```

Apple:
```
170 HOME:PRINT:PRINT:RETURN
```

Spectrum:
```
40 LET F=INT(RND*33+1)
50 LET X(J)=VAL(W$(F))
180 DIM F$(6,8):DIM N(6):DIM X(3)
```

TRS-80:
```
40 LET F=INT(RND(0)*33+1)
```

*Extended BASIC version

Puzzle answers

Pages 4-5
How many?
The words which could accompany the numbers are as follows: Hours by aeroplane (1), hours by car (5), kilometers (200), miles (125).
Hundreds and thousands
1. 2233
2. 13
3. 900
4. The 2 on the left means 2000, and the 2 on the right means 2.

Pages 6-7
Brainteasers
0.8 is bigger than 0.396.
0.5, 0.50 and 0.500 all represent the same quantity. The extra noughts merely indicate that the number is exactly 0.5.
Rounding off
2400, 7.22
Dividing by decimals
Although it looks as though the decimal point moves, it is of course the numbers which change position.

Pages 8-9
Sums with negative numbers
$6 - 2 = 4$, $^-7 + 4 = ^-3$, $2 \times ^-3 = ^-6$, $^-4 \times ^-2 = 8$, and $1 \times 3 = 3$.
Vectors
Vector B is $\begin{pmatrix} ^-6 \\ 4 \end{pmatrix}$, Vector C is $\begin{pmatrix} 8 \\ ^-3 \end{pmatrix}$.

Pages 10-11
2, 4 and 8
$128 \div 8 = 16$
Multiply by 9
Yes, 684 is divisible by 9
($6 + 8 + 4 = 18$ and $1 + 8 = 9$).
Multiply by 10
To multiply by 1000, add three noughts.
Multiply by 15
a) 120, b) 540, c) 1380
Beat the teacher
Write the sum down twice, forwards and backwards, and add downwards:

$$\begin{array}{ccccccc} 1 + & 2 + & 3 + \dots + & 998 + & 999 + & 1000 \\ 1000 + & 999 + & 998 + \dots + & 3 + & 2 + & 1 \end{array} +$$

$$1001 + 1001 + 1001 + \dots + 1001 + 1001 + 1001$$

Twice the sum of the number is $1000 \times 1001 = 1001000$ so the answer is 500500.

Pages 12-13
Classifying shapes
The building shown is called the Pentagon because it has five sides.
Regular polygons
A shape would need an infinite number of sides before it became a circle.
The family of triangles
It is not possible to draw a triangle whose sides are 5cm, 3cm and 9cm, because the length of the third side must be less than the sum of the other two sides.

Fitting shapes
The tessellation is made up of regular triangles, squares and hexagons.

Pages 14-15
Rectangular areas
$A_r = 1 \times w$ means that the area of a rectangle = length × width.
Sports centre puzzle
One way to find the area of this plan of a sports centre would be to divide it into two rectangles and a triangle. You could then use the relevant formulae to calculate the separate sections, and add them together.

Pages 17
If you sliced the cone straight down from its tip to the middle of its base, its cross-section would be a triangle (this is not, of course, a curve).

Pages 18-19
The two lines are the same length, but the arrow tips make the first line look longer.

Calculating volume
The shape on the left is 17cm^3 and the shape on the right is 14cm^3.
To find the cylinder's volume, multiply πr^2 by its height. So the formula is $\pi r^2 h$.
Building cubes
Shape 5 is left over.

Pages 20-21
Angles inside a polygon
A regular hexagon has six equal angles, so each angle would be $\frac{720}{6} = 120°$.

Angles on a straight line
$c = 180° - 110° = 70°$
Alternate angles theorem
$A\hat{C}B + A\hat{C}D = 180°$ because DCB is a straight line. $D\hat{C}E + A\hat{C}D = 180°$ because ACE is also a straight line. So $A\hat{C}B = D\hat{C}E$.
Exterior angle theorem
$\hat{E} + \hat{A} + A\hat{D}E = 180°$ because the three angles form a triangle. $\hat{E} + D\hat{E}G = 180°$ because they form the straight line AEG. So $D\hat{E}G = \hat{A} + A\hat{D}E$.
Bearings and navigation
The barge is travelling on a bearing of 317°, the cruiser on a bearing of 251°, and the plane on a bearing of 68°.

Page 23
Networks A, B, F and G are traversable.

Page 24
Sizing up fractions
⅓ is bigger than ⅟₁₀th.
Percentages
1. Astor will have 12 solars interest after one year.
2. After one year, he has 132 solars, so after two years he has
$$132 + \frac{132}{10} = 145.2 \text{ solars}$$
3. Astor will save 48 solars on the original price of the space suit.
4. $240 \times 80\% = 192$ solars.

Pages 26-27
Betting odds
If you put 8 tokens on Terror you would win 100 tokens if Terror came in first. So 1 token would win you $\frac{100}{8} = 12.5$ tokens.

Map scales
1m on the map would represent 2500 m.

Puzzles
It is bottle B's volume which is twice the size of bottle A: its height is only one dimension.

No – you would get 8 ($2 \times 2 \times 2$) times the number of biscuits in the second jar: 400 biscuits.

Pythagoras' theorem
The triangle with sides 9, 12 and 15 has a right angle because $9^2 + 12^2 = 15^2$.

Pages 28-29
Set C = the set of those shapes with three sides (triangles).
Set D = the set of shapes which have four sides (quadrilaterals).
$A \cap B = \{d\}$; i.e. d is in both A and B so n $(A \cap B)$ = 1.
$A \cup B = \{a,b,d,f,h,j\}$; i.e. the members which are in either A or B so n $(A \cup B)$ = 6.

Odd one out
There are often several possibilities for an odd one out in a set. In this case, it could be the circle (the others have straight sides), or the cube (it is a three-dimensional shape).

Venn diagrams
$A \cap B \cap C = \emptyset$

Journey puzzle
Hong Kong and Delhi and either London or Paris, and New York.

Pages 30-31
Pie chart
The other angles, to the nearest whole number, are as follows:

French = $\frac{108}{500} \times 360° = 78°$

Germans = $\frac{100}{500} \times 360° = 72°$

British = $\frac{92}{500} \times 360° = 66°$

Other = $\frac{75}{500} \times 360° = 54°$

You can check that you have calculated correctly by adding the value of the sections up and checking that they total 360°.

Scatter graph
This graph shows that most money is spent by the people in the middle-age bracket.
Mean, mode and median
Mean = 350, Mode = 380, Median = 365.
Statistics don't lie . . .
The graph on the right has a smaller gap between 1984 and 1985 which makes it appear that the time lapse is less.

Pages 32-33
The co-ordinate system
The old lady is C, the child is A, and the man is B.
Angie won the race, but the graph also shows that Billy was leading early on in the race.
Plotting Graphs
The co-ordinates are (1,6), (2,3), (3,1), (4,1), (5,3) and (6,2).
Picture Puzzle
Picture 2: 11 o'clock, picture 3: 7, and picture 5: 9.

Pages 34-35
Describing relationships
A is y = 3x, B is 10 – x, C is x + 7

Pages 36-37
The angle shown is 100°.

Pages 38-39
Powers
$2^3 = 2 \times 2 \times 2 = 8$
$2^7 \times 2^2 = 2^9$
$10^{-5} = \frac{1}{10^5}$
Standard form
7.84×10^{11}
7.62453×10^{-7}
Spotting prime numbers
2, 3, 5, 7 and 11 divide into any number under 169 (or 13^2; the next prime number after 11), except a prime number. So you can use the first five prime numbers to find any prime number up to the square of the sixth prime number, and so on.

Pages 40-41
$37_{\text{base ten}}$ is $100101_{\text{base two}}$.
$1100101_{\text{base two}}$ is $101_{\text{base ten}}$.
One less puzzle
Each column heading in binary is one more than the sum of all the headings before it. So, in this case, double 64 and take 1 from it.
Computer messages
The number should read 111000111111000.
If you sent just one redundant figure, you would know when there was an error, but you would not know how to correct it.
Other bases
1920 seconds is 32 minutes.

Page 44
Matching birth signs
In this puzzle, the result depends upon a series of events occurring, so all the stages are multiplied together.

Index

PRINTED IN BELGIUM